Deliverance

POEMS BY

Paul Kloschinsky

CANADIAN MENTAL HEALTH ASSOC.
DELTA BRANCH
#14 - 1835 - 56th Street
Delta, BC   V4L 2L8
Ph: 604-943-1878 Fax: 948-1479
e-mail: cmha.delta@dccnet.com
www.cmhadeltabranch.ca

Note for Librarians: A cataloguing record for this book is available from Library and Archives
Canada at www.collectionscanada.ca/amicus/index-e.html
ISBN 1-4251-1731-7

Printed in Victoria, BC, Canada. Printed on paper with minimum 30% recycled fibre.
Trafford's print shop runs on "green energy" from solar, wind and other environmentally-friendly power sources.

Offices in Canada, USA, Ireland and UK

Book sales for North America and international:
Trafford Publishing, 6E–2333 Government St.,
Victoria, BC V8T 4P4 CANADA
phone 250 383 6864 (toll-free 1 888 232 4444)
fax 250 383 6804; email to orders@trafford.com
Book sales in Europe:
Trafford Publishing (UK) Limited, 9 Park End Street, 2nd Floor
Oxford, UK OX1 1HH UNITED KINGDOM
phone +44 (0)1865 722 113 (local rate 0845 230 9601)
facsimile +44 (0)1865 722 868; info.uk@trafford.com
Order online at:
trafford.com/07-0101

10 9 8 7 6 5 4 3 2

To the gods, for delivering me

Success

Success is a fickle mistress.
She'll kiss you when you're sleeping,
bless your dreams with accolades,
then leave you struggle in the morning.
With the vanquished on the battlefield,
the lunatic strapped to his bed,
the rejected lover wandering the streets,
the failed athlete licking his wounds.
Until like the glory of the dawn
she'll throw you a few scraps
of your happiness,
to melt the frost
of a winter's chill
and let you dream about
her tender arms around your neck
and the blossoming spring eyes
of acceptance.

The Unknown Poet

I write my verse for the lone watchman
guarding the gates of paradise.
Crafting my lines to secure a place

beyond the killings, rejection slips,
and cigarette butts of everyday mundane

existence. Etching my rhyme on columns of smoke
rising to meet an angel's glance.
Penetrating deep into the heart of solitude,

the words of others my only nourishment,
with dreams thrown out like dirty dishwater,

and wasted words blown around like
autumn leaves. Taking sanctuary in a distant light,
a forlorn star for an unknown poet.

The Slow Journey to Recovery

I came to their house suddenly,
demanding to speak to the wife,
the husband protesting adamantly
until they finally called the police.

(At first they were completely chaotic,
the four voices of the quartet.
Each singing out of tune,
with no underlying cohesion at all.)

The mixture was as cloudy as a mudslide,
making the world seem dark and stale.
Condemning all who saw through it
to heavy thoughts and despair.

At the hospital they gave me medicine
and calmed down my rage.
But still thoughts of her filled my mind,
and I longed to talk to her one more time.

(Slowly the four singers found common ground,
occasional bouts of harmony breaking through the confusion,
until finally they hit their stride,
making music out of chaos.)

It was decided to add a compound

to the foul, cloudy mixture.
Attempting to clear it up
and release those doomed to peer through it.

After release from the hospital
I saw her one more time.
We had a heartfelt discussion
and sowed seeds for the future.

(Now they perform widely.
Drawing praise for their fluid harmonies.
Each one interacting with the others
in perfect unison and sweet music.)

The compound cleared the mixture
after two weeks of deadening despair
until it was clear as crisp water
allowing all who peered through it health and happiness.

Redemption

My problems were too extensive,
my sorrow too deep,
for me to see
anyway out
if it had to be
by myself
and my own recourses.
So that I felt lost,
cut off from
the life around me.
Destined to suffer
for the rest of my life.

Then one day
by the occurence
of some chance circumstance
and inner feelings
of peace and contentment
I felt touched
by a power
greater than myself.
With enough power and wisdom
to help me through the desolation,
like the buoys and beacons
guiding the sailboats
to safe harbors.
And leave me working
with this great navigator
at this project called my life.

Stature

I walk amongst giants.
Those who tower in stature,
whose words and music have outlasted
even the mighty redwood.
But what am I to do?
A young seedling at the foot of kings
straining for a glimpse of the light.
Fledging on moss covered ground
and all I can do is grow, grow
and push upwards in the darkness
praying for a glimpse of the light
to show me the way.
Am I a weed, a rose, a redwood?
I do not know.
But as long as I am alive
I shall grow, grow
and aim towards the bright light of recognition.

Gracefully

I woke up this morning
looked in the mirror
and realized my youth was gone,
disintegrating like butter
melting in a frying pan.
I realized my friends were busy
with their marriages,
their children,
their jobs,
no longer able to sit at the beach
around a bonfire,
singing songs
until the wee hours of the night.

I felt sad.
My sun now at it's zenith,
blazing bright at high noon,
and will soon start descending
to a glorious sunset.
I vowed to embrace the stages
of life gracefully;
the security,
maturity,
and wisdom
of advancing years
comforting me as I march onwards
towards the end of this mortal existence.

Starting Gate

I feel like a race horse
stuck in the stable.
A cramped, boring place
eating,
relaxing,
reflecting
while every once
and a while
they come by
and say
"We're about to take you
    to the starting gate."

But then the days go by
and nothing happens
and I fear I'm destined
to be a work horse
sent out to the fields
to toil and sweat.
So I just wait and pray
that some day
I'll be able to start the race.
I don't think
about if I'll win
or the winner's circle.

I just want a chance to try
and desperately want a shot
at the starting gate.

Crazy

I hope I don't seem odd to you
even though I scribble outside the lines.
I don't mean to be inappropriate,
like a lunatic pushing his shopping cart,
but rather to be original;
like a fresh, new snowflake.

So don't mistake my independence for insanity,
even though I've had bouts of madness.
But now that it has been tidied up
I still speak my mind,
shun conventions that don't fit,
only take off my hat to those I respect,
and fiercely defend my right
to dance to my chosen tune.

So don't call me crazy,
but rather see me as a rare, wild cactus
blossoming under the desert sun.

Work

They say I should do some,
though I say I already am.
Their work is visible, measurable.
Mine is for the most part hidden
until I present it to the world
and can measure my rejection slips.
But until I get that acceptance
I must pay homage to their gods
of commerce, industry and utility,
not allowed to declare myself
a traveller down a different path
where truth and beauty are honored.
No, I must secretly journey down
this desired path at night, and give
my daylight hours to more sensible pursuits
until one day I trade my stethoscope
for a pen, and walk straight on
into the night, never looking back again.

Opportunity

I wait patiently by the door,
listening for the gods to knock,
and hear nothing.

Some say I should seize the day
and create my own rewards,
but I sit still like an archer
whose targets are shrouded in fog.

So I sit waiting for God, fate,
or a turn of good weather
to blow the mist clear revealing my goal.

So I can then at least prime my bow
take aim at my future,
and like a lover rush to meet
the gods of opportunity.

In Homage to Dylan Thomas

It took a master.
I was sitting drinking
pint after pint
in the local saloon,
eying the waitress,
when they suddenly
called me a cab
and asked to leave.
Stumbling around
like a boxer
with too many blows
to the head
I reluctantly left
but in a stroke of genius
decided to come back
for another one.

That's when a met
the Apollonian peace officers.

After joking and arguing
for a few minutes
they decided to
handcuff me
and throw me in
the drunk tank.

Sitting in the tiny cell

the four walls towering
like Greek monuments
it was then that I realized
that the waitress was
a bit trickier than I had
bargained for.

And I knew that failing her
I always had the leak
from the copious pints
in the back alley afterwards
but it took a master
to whip up my triumph
like Dylan Thomas
on a good day
stumbling like
a caged Dionysus
in the drunk tank.

The Diseased Branch

This challenge to my robustness,
the branching incisive carcinoma.
Blocking my growth
at every turn.
Condemning me to obscurity,
confining me to mediocrity,
like a sharp steel blade.
Cutting up my dreams
into howling morsels,
driving my wild, weeded growth
down to diseased depths.
A scourge on my soul,
a diseased branch
condemning the organism
to tortured frustration
unless some divine hand
can gently tease it apart
and prune my spirit
from this festering poison.

Cactus

A sorrowful sundown sets this evening.
The crimson skies fading slowly.
The echo of the bright day before
lost forever in the ash of dusk.

Like the memories of my ambition
and my drive for my future
once galvanized like the sprouting seed
pushing upward towards sun and sky.

Until coming forth or confined
it meets with its destiny.
The rains falling and nourishing my soul,
a gamble on grey, bloated clouds.

Releasing its embrace on my dreams,
thirsty but now dry as a cactus.
Surviving scorched and prudent
under hot, cloudless skies.

My heart weeps for the touch
of sweet recognition and encouragement,
promising that after the last
frail sunlight of sunset fades,

and the cold night takes hold,
leaving me drifting on troubled seas,
a new day will eventually dawn
shining down with sun and rain.

Reviving the germ of my purpose,
stopping the sobs of frustration,
and releasing the glory of growth
of the goals of my organic soul.

The Wind through the Treetops

I see the wind
rustle through the treetops,
and the mountain tops
kiss the sky.
The forged faces of granite
carved by the crush of ages.
Reflecting the face of God
with the snowcaps and glaciers
creeping down the mountain sides
in slow intercourse with each other;
and the pine trees-
each individual,
each free,
like each rightful individual;
surrounded by the majesty
and carved by the glory
of life's ebb and flow.

Nighttime Stars

I was dragged from my home
and cast out into the desolate desert,
where I wandered around
chasing mirages of palm trees
and cool, crisp water.
On the horizon the smoke
of distant factories,
obliterated the nighttime stars,
the moon a pale orb,
its features all but diminished,
its light a faint flicker,
and death all around
in this barren wasteland.

Until one morning
the sun broke through the smoke
and I saw a flickering white mare
emerging from the haze on the horizon.
And it came to me.
Mounting it I fled
to where desert meets sea
and I dived in the water,
the tides carrying me away,
until I washed up on the shore
and people greeted me once again.

In Lieu of Love

I couldn't take it any more.
The long, lonely times of
nocturnal yearnings
and self satisfaction
led me stiffen up
and call the agency.

Soon thereafter she arrived
at my door. Dressed as
raw as fishnet stockings,
with wild red hair,
searing red lips
and considerable cleavage.
A weathered, aged seductress,
hardened by the years,
who approached youth in
the dim light.

And with guts to burn to
come see me in the middle
of the night.

After introductions we retired
to the bedroom and she had
her way with me.
Although not nourishing what
my soul really needed I did receive
carnal gratification.

Afterwards she asked me what I did
and I told her I wrote poems.

"e.e. cummings" is my favorite poet she said.

I then offered to give her
my first book of poems,
and signed and dedicated
her copy.

"You have the life of my dreams", she said.

"It takes a lot of work" I said to the poor
fallen soul.

She then gave my a nice hug and thanked me.
Then I let her out the door
and she was gone,
this child who had strayed
far too far from home
and can now never get back.

Crucifix

Can I take the crucifix from around your neck?
Wrap it up and gently put it away.
For tonight wild horses rear their heads
and the weeds whisper their wild siren call.
So come with me under the cloak of darkness,
to revel under crimson skies,
until like a glowing roman candle
our passion extinguishes itself;
and with one long, sweet goodbye
we brace ourselves against the dawn.

Conflict

Why do you attack me
with your biting remarks?
Is it because you don't like me,
or that I don't
do as you say
like a private
following his drill sergeant.
Can I not follow my own opinion
and make my own mistakes
like a young duckling
stumbling his way through the world.
So try to be gentle
and forgive me my errant ways,
and remember that for all my mistakes
its only life.

Family Doctor

She works hard.
Long hours sympathizing
with even the most trivial complaints.
You first meet her
in the warm receptionist
she chose.
Later in the anatomy charts,
examining tables,
speculums and stethoscopes
which adorn her rooms.
The tools of a sorceress
prescribing her spells -
don't smoke, eat right, exercise
and other specific remedies
as the situation requires.

But can she heal my deepest wounds
inflicted by the hands of fate,
God's joke on me.
Anti-depressants she might say
but they have never worked for me
so I say thank you and goodbye
and close the door
into the winter rain.

Vocation

I don't know what to do.
I went to the distinguished institutions
and earned my marketable degrees,
embarked upon a career,
but now I find the job
fits me like clothes I've since outgrown
and I'm tempted to throw them off
but having no clear choice
of new well fitting garments,
that wed desire with ability,
to put on in its place,
I'm still afraid to stand naked
striped of my social identity
so instead I write verse
and hope it spins a well fitting suit
to replace the tattered clothes
I put on in my youth.

Choice

Did you ever have to choose
                    between foul tasting medicine
         and a delectable sweet?
                                             I did.
And when faced with such a dilemma
                    I chose the candy
         and healed by Nature's loving hand.

Parents

They give you life.
Their moment of passion
transformed into your very existence.
Perhaps you came too early.
Too late.
But be grateful that you
came at all.
Notwithstanding they love you,
feed you, clothe you, teach you.
The mysteries of life unfolded
as the years march on.
And you misunderstand them
a thousand times,
until lusting for independence
you leave them.
Perhaps you stay there,
or perhaps life molests you
and you end up back in their home
and they nurture you again
with a love and support
like you've never known elsewhere.
And you want to thank them
but you know the best way
is to do the same for your children,
and you pray that they remain
alive and well for a long time.

Personals

I need a woman.
Not just any woman.
One with a heart that's strong,
holding firm in the face of ill fortune.
One with a mind that's curious,
probing deeply the inexhaustible
realm of knowledge.
One with a soul that's deep
with possibilities and hidden delights.
One with a spirit that soars,
overcoming any adversity.
One with a fair disposition,
pleasing to the eye,
though not necessarily perfect.
And if I meet such a woman
I would match her virtue,
like two poker players
raising each other's bet,
until if successful
we are both declared winners
and share the bounty
of lasting relationship.

Eden

Writing is a weakness
practiced under the moonlight,
as wild dogs howl
and the weeds softly sway
on unkempt graves
for lost loves,
forgotten dreams,
unsatisfactory childhoods,
and vague yearnings
for a forgotten paradise.
The garden of Eden.
Sometimes vaguely remembered
in morning traffic
as the radio reports
the latest technological advance
or murderous spree.

Embrace

Making love to you is like coming home
to the place I really belong.
The earth opens up
its depths embrace me
and Nature completes me
in your arms.

Balance

I'm crucified between desire and duty.
The eternal pull of wild gratification
nails me to the cross of my ought to be's,
leaving me to search for some balance,
a fulcrum to rest the conflicting armies of my soul,
in some peace that spares my dreams,
lets them soar like an eagle,
but can they stand even stand erect
or will reality murder them in their cradle?

Surgical Love

Can I make an incision in your thorax?
Excise your heart.
Anastamose it to my own,
cauterizing any bleeding feelings
of doubt or confusion;
using broad spectrum Ancef
to eradicate any thoughts
of historical lovers.
Suturing your flesh to mine.
Healing the gaping wound of our separation,
letting us lye post-operatively in the same bed,
permanently approximated.

Psychiatrist

I used to be like him
watching the mass of humanity
parade before my eyes.
Trying to make sense of it all-
classify, predict, treat.
But that was taken from me
and now I am just one
of the multitudes that see him.

And he listens and observes,
prescribing various combinations of pills,
until finally after this roulette wheel therapeutics
I can say I really feel well again.
But we don't really discuss
my needs and dreams
or what I want to do
with this new found sanity.
So I keep my wishes to myself,
even though they could use a friend,
and give thanks for his biological competence;
and hope one day I can show him
I'm a significant man in my own right.

Daybreak

The birds start it off.
Filling nature with their song.
While the sunrise is still
eagerly anticipated
and the rest of the world sleeps.
Then finally the light seeps
in from the eastern horizon,
the sky becoming stained in pink.
Heralding the mighty sun's return
which like spring
is a new beginning.
For the commuters leaving their homes
and driving in their cars.
And for those troubled souls
in need of redemption
who pray for a bright sunny day
to end the incessant drizzle
of their current life.

Tree

It stands there tall and frosted.
Branching out like a good argument.
It's leaves have long since fallen
and now a dusting of snow
adorns it's branches.
Producing a symmetry and grace
which can only be seen as sublime.
Giving a glimpse beyond
this mortal existence
into the divine mind.
Whether that be the Creator
or the forces behind the random
mutations of DNA,
it is clear that
not only function,
but also beauty,
reigned supreme in it's design.
And faced with this majesty
it is hard to consider
life is all one big fluke.

Devotion

Hold on; hold on true and firm.
While vicissitude dumps what it may
and the night calls forth some forbidden desire.
Cling to the inner fiber of your heart,
like the pilgrims at the harvest feast,
with a tenacity that never yields
to bring forth in measures of years not days
the fruits of love's oak.
With bonds that weather storms
and brace oneself
against the deep, dark beyond.

The New Priests

The catechism of the medical fundamentalists,
the new priests and shamans,
tyrants against hedonism-
the sweet elixir of life.
Casting their curse on the fairest pleasures,
thinking they hold eternal life in their hands,
when all along
God decides whether you live or die,
and eternal life is in His hands.

Creator

A midsummer's night blankets the sky,
the fading sun drifting towards the horizon,
a breeze gently blowing,
the birds softly chirping,
and I sit wondering whether a Creator
sketched this masterpiece
or whether the random unfolding
of the universe etched such a scene.
I do know if God did lend His hand
He will not reveal this this to me
in any way irrefutable.
So I'm left to sit and ponder
at the improbable twists of fate
and the driving force behind this budding rose.

Ethics

I was wandering through the forest
torn from side to side
by visions of dancing girls,
my family, my friends,
my occupation,
and the siren call of fallen women.
Until not knowing which way to step
I met a little dwarf
hidden beneath a grassy knoll
and he said,
"Evil?
Evil is heartless cruelty
and for those who know,
everything is permitted
with compassion."
So I just smiled
and went along my merry way
and let my heart have its say.

Unconscious Sources

I read the great psychologists
talk of Id and Egos
and shadows and Selfs,
until confused and drifting
a simple thought did strike me
that God lives in your unconscious.

As natural as a duck paddling
on the water,
or the wind catching a sail,
and we're all surrounded within
and without by the Lord,
the divine hermaphrodite,
who inserts timely thoughts and memories
nurturing, provocative, hostile
depending upon the inclination,
be it a Freudian slip
or rapture,
He's always there guiding and developing
His divine creation and plan
until He greets us in eternity.

Dreams

My dreams are like flowing water
running down a mountain side
rushing onward to their goal
accumulating persistently if blocked
either removing the obstacle
or finding a new way onward.
Flowing around the stoppage
and moving on to the ocean
gratified at last.

Truth

"Everything happens for a reason"
I heard someone say
and as I looked around
it seemed to me
that the hand of God
is sometimes clenched like a fist:
terminal illness,
violent death,
natural disasters,
insanity,
all suggest a truth
whose hard cutting edge
will always offend sensibilities;
until you know the big picture
which I hope is God's specialty.

Return

I've tried to forget my dreams
lock them away in safety deposit box,
tuck them away to be retrieved
at some later, yet to be determined date.
But they don't rest quietly
and break out of their prison
like some resourceful, clever prisoner.

They invade my room,
and my thoughts,
like floodwater seeping into a house,
until they upset my safe plans,
disturbing them like roots
through the pavement.
Leaving me to cling
to the remaining scraps
of my orderly life
and hope that out of my
desperation is born,
like a caterpillar metamorphosing
into a butterfly,
a new, robust life.

Belief

I'm sorry I ever doubted you
when you sang my praises
saying I am
who I want to be.
But I doubted you
believing it too good to be true,
like a bride at the alter.
So I wrapped myself in my despair,
like a sleeping bag in arctic winds,
oblivious to the coming thaw.
Until I found myself lying
in a warm, summer meadow
and realized that all along
you were right as the summer sun.

Pagan

I don't believe in any organized religion
but I do believe in God.
A divinity as pure and natural
as a mountain stream.
I am a committed hedonist
but also believe in love and compassion,
and abhor self destruction.
In short I am a heathen,
a noble savage,
and I challenge you
with your creeds and codes
to be any more exalted
than me.

Enlightenment

Like a blind man with a cane
I stumbled around this earth
unaware of the prevailing winds
and currents.
Until one day I was struck by lightening
and my sight returned
and I saw the unseen forces
that guide men's lives.
I realized that for the good hearted
there is nothing to fear
if they give control
over to a higher power,
a divinity as solid and reliable
as the earth we walk upon.
So I sipped from the grail
and my deepest wish was thus fulfilled.

Worship

I heard the church-bells ring
and I went inside to hear a sermon.
It was all about sinners and eternal damnation.
I found it a most droll and boring affair
so I left quietly.
I sought out these sinners,
the sexual ones at least,
and joined them in orgiastic worship
of the male and female deities
and their ecstatic union.
We became a cult of fertility,
honoring the bounty of Nature,
and the self renewing rites of spring.

Deliverance

I have been rescued
like a man lost in the forest.
Hungry, cold and alone
whose only hope of rescue has vanished.
Until one day he hears the sound of
helicopter blades overhead
and rushes to a clearing
into the arms of his rescuers.
Later fed, warm and in bed
he marvels at his unexpected miracle.

Like him I too have been saved
by some timely, kind remarks
and the judicious use of antidepressants,
and marvel at the lifting
of the crushing pain in my heart
and my newfound optimism about the future;
that is as sweet and beautiful as a rainbow.

Treasure

I went looking for my happiness,
traveling far and wide
over mountains and streams,
under bridges,
and I found nothing.
Until I cursed the fates
and pissed in the wind
for leaving me in such a forlorn state,
yearning for more than life can give.

Then one day I stumbled home,
looked at the familiar surroundings,
my loved ones drawn near,
and like a man looking for his glasses
only to discover they are already on his head,
I realized I had all I needed right there
and found my elusive treasure after all.

Jailbreak

Who would have believed
a pill could have busted me
out of hell.
For try as I might
with thoughts,
behaviors, and
personal contact
to lyse my foul moods
they did not work
in any appreciable sense;
but taking a tiny tablet
achieved so much more
cutting me out
of the belly of the whale
and enabling me
to sing again.

Moth

I'm drawn to you
like a moth to a flame.
Over and over again
I come at you
and I fear I might get burnt
if I fly too close
but then you reassure me
it won't happen.

Sometimes I drift away
fumbling in the darkness,
but soon thereafter
I return once again
to your heat,
and radiance.
Being insatiable
for your wisdom.
So I will flutter around you
until I perish
and then become one
with your flame
for all eternity.

A Ring brought Forth

Its not that hard to understand
What flesh does desire can't be denied
A ring brought forth from pagan lands.

A civilization built on moral bricks
Must tremble and shake at the sight of this
The sartyr's song will make them sick.

Hark back to the age where Dionysus ruled
Love flowed freely and hearts were full
Then the savior came and things were cooled.

Why must a heart that flows be necessarily opposed
Must compassion's face be so devoid
Of passion's fire and blooming rose.

To see the Creator's hand in a grain of sand
And in every desire from a healthy heart
A ring brought forth from pagan lands.

State of Grace

Its really quite difficult to achieve.
Though some would say they have the answer
with their affirmations and steps.
However my experience
has been one of profound suffering,
like the grief of losing a loved one
over and over again.
And it seems to lead nowhere,
and you think you just can't endure,
and it strips you of your faith.

Then after you've gone far
past the point of no return
one day you say a simple belief in God,
even though you have considerable doubts,
and a feeling of well being and grace
descends upon you like warm, spring rain
and it feels too right not to be
something that you can bank on.
And you can believe that this
is not a cold, unfeeling universe
but rather the cherished creation
of a caring God.

Who has His own way of nurturing
His beloved creations.

On it's Head

The sinners are saints,
the saints are sinners.
Difficult to comprehend
if you're just a beginner.

The sinners are saints,
the saints are sinners.
Pay attention closely
if you want to be a winner.

Once there was a time
when they didn't know of sin.
Their gods were holy
even though they frequently sinned.

Then the cross came and
turned the truth on its head,
elevating the persecutor, and damning
the sinner, even after he's dead.

Now desires as natural
as a clear mountain stream
are cursed by the saints
leaving one with just dreams.

So take a chance and find a way
between the saint's compassion
and that other affair of the heart-
the sinner's passion.

The sinners are saints,
the saints are sinners.
Do you see it now? The
dividing line is getting thinner.

Humor

As far as I can see
its a totally overlooked
aspect of divinity.
However, it seems implausible
that the Creator of
earth and the heavens
would not also have
created and possess
a sense of humor.

The much cherished
and medicinal qualities
of a good joke
must not be lost on God,
and perhaps He can
laugh with us at our
stupidest, most self depreciating jokes
that put things into perspective,
wed parody and irony,
and provide
the welcome release
of a good
punch-line.

A Dying Breed

In a world such as this
where the evening news bombards you
with every imaginable depravity
it takes a unique wide eyed wonderment
to believe in the goodness of humanity
and even a greater marvel to believe
in a good, caring God.
But it is precisely these people
who can be counted as the true believers
those without sin, cynicism and with good hearts
that keep the torch burning
because in this vanishing kind,
who refuse to be tainted by experience,
innocence is faith.

A Place I Know

I sometimes go somewhere I know,
a place kings and queens
will never know.
Its a place few will ever see
though they travel far and wide.
How I found it I'll never know.
They keep it under lock and key
and though there's no password to get in
you must be initiated to enter.
And like baroque music
in a world full of pop
it refreshes the soul
with ancient remedies
leaving you ready
to take on what you must
this sacred place
they hold in trust.

Peace

In this world of turmoil,
that assaults you at every turn,
leaving you anxious and perplexed
unable to find a moment's peace
let alone a lasting serenity
that supports your daily life.
In this world I have found
one thing that helps quiet the noise
and that is faith
in a good God,
in a caring God,
the defender of the good hearted.
Bestowing a wisdom and understanding
few ever receive on earth.
For it is only with this faith
that the troubles of the world
are deflected like rain
from an umbrella
and a true joy springs forth
from divine love.

Judgement Day

They say its coming,
as every person
pushing a shopping cart
with all their belongings
through city streets
knows all too well.

As night seeps in
casting shadows that
elongate and coalesce;
and the bitter cold wraps
you tight, burning
like a thousand tiny pinches;
and a page from
yesterday's newspaper
gets blown up in your face.

It occurs now that you're naked,
standing alone,
every possession stripped
from you, peeled away
like your youth and vigor.

And when they come for you,
shivering and frightened as
you are, the one thing they
want to know, the one thing
that will sort your fate is -

Does anyone love this person?

Beating the Odds

His influence is barely perceived
and you just might miss it
unless you pick up
on the subtle signs
that happen as chance occurence
when you beat the odds
and cash in on a small miracle.

Its only then that we realize
the depth of His concern for us
for in the presence of a gift
that answers our innermost wishes
we find the answers to our prayers
and take a step, however small
towards becoming the person
we were truly meant to be.

Machine

It functions so efficiently,
calculating and sorting and searching.
Doing exactly what it is told to do,
and it never complains
unlike the humans we expect
to function in a similar fashion.
Of course some are prone to organization
and function easily this way.
But then there are the ones who do not,
the ones who cannot organize themselves
to work like a machine,
the ones who dream of natural rhythms
and products that may be
beautiful but less then efficient.
Its hard for these people
to find a place outside of industrialization,
where they can do their work,
like a dandelion sprouting
through a crack in the highway,
and find some peace
in the middle of the churning machine.

Left Alone

Most do their best
to avoid it.
Clinging,
like a child to their mother,
to contact,
any contact,
rather than face it.

And of course
our families,
our psychiatry,
our society
marks our social successes
as the sole indicator
of how we are doing.

Well, I have fallen
in love with solitude.
I don't care that people
talk and give me their
heartfelt condolences as to
how lonely I must be.

I'm not lonely.
I'm not crazy.

I find riches within myself
when alone that far outstrip

everyday contact.

So leave me be
and understand I'm doing fine
and that all things being equal
I would just rather be
left alone.

Beast

They killed it.
Tore it limb from limb,
swinging the dismembered parts
over their heads like a tomahawk.

Gone was the rage,
and jealousy,
and murderous thoughts
put to rest in the slaying
of the beast that sounds the sirens
that cut through the thick night air,
leaving children orphans
and nations vanquished.
Until as the blood issued forth,
like the eruption of a volcano,
from the sacrificial brute,
they were released
from the animal tension;
able to live free
ecstatic and wild.

Grip

He grips me like an ice-pick
being applied to my stomach.
Demanding all sorts of things -
stop being unique,
stop being creative;
because he is afraid,
so very afraid,
of the things he doesn't understand.

In far off places
he has purged societies
of the gifted and the intelligent.

But for me he just sends me
waves of terror,
demanding his way,
though he knows
as well as I
he will never get it.

Apollo

They scurry about in their white coats,
symbolizing their purity
and perfection.
And they try to remove
all imperfections
in their patient's bodies.
Though it seems to me
that the imperfections
where put their by God,
and do not lend themselves
as easily to pruning
as a garden shrub.
And though they have a few remedies
most peoples' problems
stain their white coats
with bloody honesty.

Moralist

He gets you when you
least expect him.
Lurking in the shadows,
applying his cherished
book of rules –
cursing the greatest joys
and the smallest delights.
Urging you to raise your standards
to clear his ever rising hurdles
until devoid of life
you face the final judgment
and are denied entrance
to the gates of paradise
it being a place reserved
for those who can enjoy themselves.

Winter

There doesn't seem to be much alive
in this barren landscape.
The trees stand naked
stripped of their once proud foliage,
which now lies reduced to ash.
The bees and other insects have perished,
and the birds have fled seeking warmer climates.
While the endless drizzle
and dark gray skies
leaves one wondering
if anything
can live here again.

If it were not for
a warm fire,
a Christmas tree,
(reminding us that some things
survive even this climate),
or a New Year's toast
one could easily think
that one's grasp on life
was as fragile as an autumn leaf.

As all is silent as a church
like one day we shall be.

And the stone cold eternity of the tomb
seems just a short time away.

Spring

We set the clocks ahead today.
And magically in the past week
Nature was transformed
from a cold, decrepit hag
to a young, robust princess
eager to sing and pollinate
as if she had put on a glass slipper
or had awoken from a slumber.

The sun also made a triumphant return
reclaiming lost territory
banishing the cold
to slender shadows under rocks.
Declaring that not only
will he be stronger
but will also stay longer,
like the promises of a returning lover;
reviving the once dead landscape
into a flourishing pastoral scene
buzzing with activity
like a fever had just broken
and Nature had been
snatched from the
jaws of death;
giving hope to
all who have died
but still live on
that the resurrection
may someday happen
to them too.

Wild

Don't try to tie me down
with your rules and expectations.
For like a dancing flame
I can't be pinned down
and change as the situation demands.

Untamable as the wind
I follow an inner course
not one that is destructive
to you or me
but rather one that is free
like the eagle, the lion, the robin
rebelling against anyone
who opposes my inner compass.

So until they lay me in my grave
I will break and bend
the conventions of society.
Gently and selectively as I see fit.
And like the surf pounding the shore
I will relentlessly chip away
at the forces that try
to keep me harmless,
and well behaved.

The Trial

I was molested in my innocent youth-
torn apart from my family, friends, and work;
cast adrift on a raging sea
with no knowledge of the prevailing winds.
Clinging to the words from a few books,
battling slippery changing beasts,
who attacked my very weakest points.
Until finally they allowed me to negotiate
and led me through years of questionable discussions;
then finally they revealed wonders I could never imagine
that I now must test on the hard rock of reality.

I Suffer Alone

I was cast adrift on a sea of confusion
with storm clouds forming over western skies.
My head full of voices,
my heart as heavy as a bowling ball,
seeking refuge in solitude.
Shooting up on Van Gogh,
mainlining a quick fix of Mozart,
writing verse like some need oxygen,
until I accumulated a stack of rejection slips;
each one like a stiletto piercing my spirit.
Until my dreams convulsed,
my heart burned like a forest fire,
and I cried out for a companion
to share my defeats
and found none;
so here I remain
suffering alone.

Cynicism

I met a man the other day
who proceeded to extol the vices of society.
The crime, corruption,
inefficient bad government,
the tedious redundancy of daily life,
the wasteland of the spiritually deprived,
and the probable downfall of it all.

I took my leave of this man politely
and proceeded to wash my face in a clear stream.
Vowing that as sure as the sun rises in the morning
and day follows night
I would see the goodness in men's hearts,
the marvel of human culture,
the freshness of each new day,
the joy of children,
and the improbable miracle
that is life itself.

Television

It sits there silent
in its sleek black casing.
It's elongated silver buttons
longing to be pushed.
It's screen looks black as night
and it promises to be a good companion.
So I take the remote
with its big red power button
and turn it on.
I'm bombarded
by news, sports,
the latest sitcoms,
and a multitude of people
entering my tiny room.

But they prove to be false companions,
for although they have plenty to say
they ask nothing about me,
nor do they care.
With the bright light
of the collective consciousness
drowning out the faint whisperings
of my own mind.
So I turn it off
and enjoy traversing
the meandering tributaries
of my own thoughts.

Stars

They lye sprinkled amongst the heavens
pinpoint lights adorning the nighttime sky.
Some are clustered in recognizable forms-
Orion, the Big Dipper, the Seven Sisters,
and I wonder if Man can make sense
out of the random outpourings of the universe
then maybe I can make sense out of the random
circumstances of my own life.
Like a sailor using a sextant
to guide him at night to welcome harbors
maybe I can guide my own life
to the places I most desire.
Instead of drifting on a sea
of random circumstance.
So I will read the heavens,
sail the social seas,
to find my final destination;
and find what I've been missing
all along.

Angel

She represents our loftiest ideals-
the small ornamental angel
with her childlike figure,
wings and bright eyes.
Perched upon her pedestal
experiencing joy, contentment,
peace, fulfillment,
love, bliss,
and I wonder if she's just
Man's wishful thinking
or God's golden promise.
A glance at the evening news
suggests she can't be found here,
but maybe she can in eternity
when God saves us
from this slaughterhouse.

Golf

Its damn hard to do
hit the little ball with a stick.
As hard as a drunk man
walking a straight line-
some can do it,
most can not.
But still they swarm
the courses in multitudes
slicing to the right,
hooking to the left.
Not a game for perfectionists;
but they try too,
obsessing over their scores
and a missed putt.

I'd like to make
the ball as big as a beach-ball
and the hole as big
as the grand canyon.
Maybe then they'd be gratified.
If that fails I'd suggest
they search real hard
for something they're really good at
and take that up instead.

Sadist

My heart burns,
yearning for something more,
fueling my dreams
from what some would call
the pleasure principle.
I wonder if God
pushes from within
maybe He controls the pleasure principle.
And if He pushes from without
maybe He controls the reality principle.
Given the gross incongruence
of these two forces in my life
I must conclude,
that like a cruel pet owner,
He is the ultimate sadist.

Desperation

She wants to kill herself,
or so she says.
She seems serious enough
with definite plans,
previous attempts,
and no shortage of tears.
She says she feels as if
her heart has been broken
and she doesn't know why.
Seriously broken it seems
aching like an ischemic limb,
wilting like a plant
someone forgot to water.
So I explore it with her,
confirming her support networks,
and give her an effective treatment,
then let her walk out the door;
into what is I hope a nurturing environment,
and pray she doesn't have the will
to carry out her plans.

Toddler

She brings smiles wherever she goes
my little curly topped niece.
A goodwill ambassador for hope
with smiles, joy
and infectious enthusiasm.
And courage too.
Taking my little finger for the first time,
walking up the stairs with me,
sitting beside me on my piano bench,
as I played her a tune.
Warming my heart
like it hasn't been in a long time,
and winning me over
with the power
of innocence.

Talent

I tried my best
and it wasn't good enough.
I have a disgusting amount of talent.
Enough to tease me,
make me think I can reach my dreams,
but in the cool light of day,
like a failed athlete stuck in the minors,
I don't have enough for success.
It makes me wonder
that maybe burning desire without enough ability
is one of God's worst jokes.

Fate

Nightfall blankets the city
and I sit pondering God,
mental illness,
and the inexplicable nature of fate.
As the city lights twinkle
in the distance
I come to the realization
that despite my best efforts
my life is almost completely
beyond my control.
As unpredictable as next week's weather.
Lying in the hands of other people
and perhaps
just maybe
in the hands of God.
As I gaze at the stars
I say a prayer
that they be positively aligned
for my eventual success.

Mystique

I wandered through the city
wounded from my broken heart,
and found strippers and prostitutes
eager to please me.
Displaying an aspect of the Goddess
found nowhere else as raw-
her sexual mystique,
electrifying touch,
and enduring power.
Leaving me hungry to possess her
but all she did was whisper to me
"In a moment of bliss
 eternity blows you a kiss".

Painter

She's a painter
but she doesn't paint.
Why I don't know.
Like a bird that refuses to fly
even though its wings are not clipped
she sits and theorizes,
waiting for divine inspiration,
instead of just picking up her brush
and doing the work.
So I gently prod her along
and hope that one day she realizes
that the greatest achievements
begin with the humblest beginnings.

Stable

I think I'm finally stable,
stable as an astronaut
under his other worldly stress.
I owe it all to you
with your sound advice,
accurate criticism,
and generous praise.
And I hope my space shuttle
can now steer true,
and I can guide it safely home
before the madness returns
with its agony
and disruption;
disturbing my chosen trajectory
in a most unstable fashion.

Motorcycle

My life has just become dangerous.
I have met a woman
with an alluring smile
and an eagle tattooed to her ass.
Unlike Ulysses
who was bound to his mast
I have heeded the siren call
embracing her enthusiastically.

My life has become
like riding a motorcycle,
fun to ride
but also risky.

Raising concerns from my loved ones
but I can't resist
to ride down the open road,
holding my wild woman,
living in the moment,
and pushing my feelings
to the limit.

Identity

I don't know who I am.
I've taken the personality tests,
dissected my temperament,
analyzed my likes
and dislikes,
and I think I now know
who I would like to be.
But I fear that that
may have nothing to do
with who I really am.
And like a private in the army
my reality is much less exciting
than my cherished dreams,
but I'll take a few steps
in my desired direction;
like a desperate pilgrim
and let fate decide.

Slumber

I thought I had put my foes to bed
and could sit up while they slept
but something stirred them from their slumber
and they joined me in my sitting room.
At first they were complimentary and sweet
but then they turned on me in an instant
attacking my disposition,
assaulting my dreams,
asserting arbitrary opinions
until I cried out for a hero
who could defeat the foul beasts,
or at least bore them with everyday life.
Until they were vanquished,
restoring my home to its serene state,
with the promise of years of peace.

Sphinx

I sought out a sphinx
with a Midas touch
who's many arms reach all of us.
I've made a few attempts
at answering it's riddle
and I fear one was correct,
but now it is too busy with other things
to concern itself with me.

Though I suspect it hasn't forgotten me
and will devour me some day
and I will turn to gold,
glimmer for a while,
be interviewed, photographed, and coddled
until I become a prisoner in my home.

Then it breathes it's fire
of scandal,
faded significance,
and advancing age
until my gold becomes covered in soot.
So I pray it doesn't find me,
although I know of no other way
to succeed.

Doctor

I hated being a family doctor
even though I tried my best,
and I fear that makes me a bad person,
like a criminal who doesn't care.
They say medicine is the noblest profession,
and that may very well be,
but the uncertainty
and indecision
I faced on a daily basis
disturbed me deeply;
and like an actor
who forgets his lines
I was afraid I'd bomb
in front of a patient
or worse still
miss something serious.
Maybe if I'd been able
to stick with it longer
I'd have developed the confidence
to find satisfaction
with the work;
or maybe I'd still dream,
like a disgruntled employee,
of a job that was truer
to my disposition.

Belonging

I don't quite fit in
with those around me.
Its not I don't love them
or have some things in common,
its just that we seem to have
fundamental differences
in temperament
and interest.
Like a man
raised by wolves
who has seen
his first human,
I know of people
who I think are like me.
The problem is
how do I meet them,
let them see who I am,
and have them hopefully
validate my nature.

Wishes

I've lost my dreams
and my faith,
like vapor diminishing
in the air.
Reality has destroyed them
and I'm devastated,
like a child
who has lost his dog,
and I'm crying inconsolably
and wondering why life
can't be more compliant
to my wishes.

Clockradio

It's bright red numbers
pierce the darkness
of my bedroom.
Relentlessly ticking off
the hours and minutes
of my life.
Which seem insignificant
in the short term,
but when they grow
to days, months, years
they carry considerably more weight.

Then it rudely awakens me
at some ungodly hour in the morning,
like some petty tyrant.
The obnoxious, irritating noise
foreshadowing how I will feel
after I shut it off.
I wish I could silence it forever,
and live and sleep to my own
and celestial rhythms.
But its hard to do in this society
unless one is fortunate enough
to be able to live and work,
like in some pre-industrial age,
free from the petty demands
of schedules and commitments.

Smile

I've stumbled through this world
on dirty, dark city streets.
I've seen thieves and murderers
as well as broken hearts.
I've heard of shooting sprees,
corruption,
and natural disasters
until my mind was full
of the dark side of life,
overflowing like some foul cauldron.

Then suddenly I opened a door,
found you sitting there,
and you flashed me a beautiful smile.
Instantaneously I forgot
about all my troubles,
like a man just released from prison,
and like a shot of morphine
my spirits lifted,
I felt no pain,
and like the resurrection
my world was redeemed.

Poker

I entered a poker game
with a most distinguished opponent
who said He was the supreme being himself.
But He cleverly kept his identity hidden
so I didn't know if he was a buffoon
whose chips were no good,
or the Creator himself.
But on we played.
He dealt the cards.
I thought I was dealt
respectable intelligence
and creative abilities.
So I put my self esteem
and livelihood on the table.
He saw my bet and raised me
publication and productivity.
I then raised him a bunch of poems.

He laughed and raised me faith.
I fumbled through my chips
unsure if I could match this bet
but then He pointed out
a chip I had overlooked
which was indeed faith.
So I called His bet.
I laid down my cards.
He laid down his
and they were my artistic recognition
and happiness.

I was declared a winner.
I breathed a sigh of relief
and marveled at this
most rewarding little game.

The Divine Jerk

I've been brutalized
and I fear its been by God.
With His endless tricks
and sleight of hand
He's left me abused and confused
like a mistreated slave.
I'm not too impressed,
and I wonder what good there can be
in a world with a Creator like this.
I hope that His games
have some beneficial reason,
perhaps to teach me
about courage and intelligence.
So all I do is pray
that He not just be the divine trickster,
and can lead me to a better place.

Hockey

They herald from the most unsung places-
weaned on frozen ponds.
Until one day they are thrust in the limelight
or else toil in the minors,
where they check, grind
shoot, skate
modern day gladiators
battling like in the Roman coliseum,
and they have the
cuts, bruises,
and missing teeth to prove it.

It strikes me
that hockey is an entertaining juxtstaposition
of grace and brutality
and on the good nights
grace wins.
And some lucky city
is given a collective shot in the arm,
and like a psychologist once told me
a heightened sense of self esteem.

Independence

I asked you for my independence
like a prisoner for parole.
You studied my request carefully
then added a few key provisions
which you thought were reasonable
but which on further review
I concluded they stifled my freedom
by not allowing me to do
what I really wanted to do.
So I wrestled with this problem,
stuck at the crossroads
between desire and duty,
and decided to do things your way.
Which diffused the situation
but left me fearful
that my heart just wilted and died
a little bit inside.

Natural

"It's very difficult to achieve"
I heard the noted psychologist say.
With superhuman efforts,
heroic struggles,
numerous trials,
glorious victories,
and moral quagmires.
All in the name
of wholeness, health
and happiness.

But I couldn't help but wonder
if a tree branches like a superman,
or a rose blooms like a hero,
or a lion has moral dilemmas
and I concluded that they did not.
This health and wholeness
so valued and praised
actually happens as naturally
as water flowing down a mountainside
with a minimum of pain
and an innocent happiness.

Airport

They come from many far off places
taxiing in from the runway.
Their varied emblems glistening in the sunlight
as they converge on the terminal
where their weary passengers disembark
and make their way to the arrivals gate.
Where they are greeted by loved ones
who kiss, hug and hold them
whether its been two days or twenty years
giving support to the adage
"absence makes the heart grow fonder"
although it is also said
"out of sight, out of mind"
but perhaps they just neglected to show up.

Soon the planes are boarded
with new passengers
and taxi and line up to take off,
going half way around the province,
country, globe.
Some shuttling south for the winter,
like migrating geese,
while others traveling to new worlds,
like Columbus of old,
where a new group of people
will display their affection
for some of the travelers,
and make this planet seem
a very small place.

The Logic of Feeling

At first it seems quite irrational
the turbulent world of emotions.
With the unpredictability of love and relationships,
the destructiveness of anger and rage,
the dehabilitating effect of fear and anxiety.
But with the right perspective
things seem predictable and rational after all.
For just as a rose blooms subject to biological law
so an emotion is governed by its own principles:

Do what you enjoy,
avoid what you don't like,
marry for love,
follow your bliss,
think realistic thoughts,
take care of yourself,
and many more.
Which all lead to a happiness
and health of feeling
that is as reliable and logical
as the latest, well engineered computer.

Highway 17

They pour along the highway,
headlights glistening in the distance,
streaming towards their destination.
I wonder where that is?
Is it to home
to the affection of loved ones?
Or to some new place
with the taste of adventure?
At any rate one thing is sure
they're heading towards their destiny.
For just as the accumulation of each day's weather
constitutes a climate,
so does the accumulation of daily events
constitutes a destiny.
Which none of us can really control
except maybe in the short term.
So I hope the drivers can navigate
the vicissitudes of their days
as surely as they steer their cars
down the open road.

Medusa

At first her hair looks so beautiful
the curly locks flowing over her shoulders.
Its only when you get closer
that you notice the snakes.

The first being irrationality.
Simply refusing to think things through
even though she possesses
considerable intelligence.
Leading her to be unpredictable
and hard to pin down.

The second being lack of empathy.
An inability to know
and care about other's feelings.
This snake has venom
with biting remarks and criticism,
which stings with intelligence.

The third being infidelity.
Leading her to cheat on her lovers.
This being particularly painful
to those who have fallen for her.

So once you have torn free of her
these snakes lead you to
pray for a hero
to slay her foul beasts.
And restore her to her place
by Athena's side.

Pandora's Box

I was innocently going
about my business
when I decided to
turn on the news.

I switched on the television
and slowly as I watched
all the demons of mankind escaped
and came screaming into my room.

(They spoke of crime, murder,
corruption, scandal,
accident, disaster,
death, and disease)

and sadly nowhere
in this mess
was to be found
hope.

So I switched it off
and went for a walk
with many foul demons
circling my head.
And as Nature chirped
and buzzed around me,
oblivious to my plight,
I found my own hope.
As fragile as a sprouting violet,

in the renewal of spring,
which lifted my spirits
and made the demons dissolve
like steam in the air.

Holocaust

I still can't believe it happened.
They taught me about it in school,
reminded me about it in the media,
and rendered it on film.
But I still think it must be a fictional nightmare.
That human beings are not capable of such things,
and I will awake and it will be a bad dream.
But then the number hits me-
six million.
Six million.
Systemically slaughtered like cattle.
All in the name of power
and purity.
I wonder if God witnessed this,
or any of the other atrocities in the world,
will he ever stop weeping,
or will he just put an end to this human experiment
sending us all packing on the road to oblivion.
But before he does
I hope he remembers the innocence of a child,
or the hope to be found
in every good, compassionate person's heart.

Inspector

He edits everything I do
criticizing this,
rejecting that.
Until I give up in frustration
or else in one last ditch effort
produce something acceptable
that I can expand upon.

"As long as its good",
he says emphatically,
like a quality control inspector
in a book factory.
Its best to keep writing
for nothing produces his fury
like a blank page.

But sometimes I freeze
before such critical thinking,
until an idea guides me along,
like the wind catching a luffing sail,
and sweeps me to my destination.
And my inspector reluctantly concludes
it was worth the journey after all.

Savior

I thought that you could save me
from the wasteland of my life.
The endless dreaming,
obstacles,
and soul searching.
I hoped you could
fulfill all my wishes,
and make me whole.
But now I realize that you cannot,
and like a man about to be executed
I now know my only hope
lies in the hands of God.

So I'm free to appreciate you
as the improbable miracle
that you are.
And let you wipe away
my boredom,
lonely nights,
and tedious arguments.
Leaving the rest for
the one who is gifted
in the art of resurrection.

Entrepreneur

I once knew a man
who thought he could do no wrong.
He acted like he had it all-
his own company,
money,
real estate,
and vision.
He thought good things were
bound to happen,
that his ship would
inevitably come in
loaded with treasure.
Like Narcissus
gazing at his own reflection
he fell in love with himself.

Now that man has fallen
on to desperate times.
His vision proving to be
too shortsighted.
I pray if I'm ever
stricken with self love
it be on sturdy foundation,
and I don't find out too late
that my vision needs
corrective lenses.

Young Love

I forgot how much you meant to me
now that there's years between us.
The fun we had,
wide eyed and intoxicated,
with the fresh luscious springtime.
Using our youth as a weapon
to dance through the minefields
of commitments and schedules.
Singing songs on the beach,
making love wherever we please.
Now though some have come
to take your place
nothing matches the simplicity
and innocence,
like a first kiss,
of our early love.

Worry

It grips you
like a straightjacket.
The endless pondering
of some future outcome,
burning like the noonday sun,
overpowering all other thoughts
like the sun the nighttime stars.
Turning it over and over again
in your strung out, weary mind.
Until finally you seize the moment
and act to influence things,
or else hopefully your intellect
realizes there's small chance of disaster
or there's nothing you can really do.
So you can move on
to more productive things
and defeat the grip
of the tyrannical thoughts.

Trouble

I'm having trouble making up my mind
between two divergent paths.
One is a continuation of my youthful choices
and leads to a well defined place.
I wonder if I have a moral responsibility
to do what I was trained to do.
The other path is a fulfillment
of my childhood dreams
and is a path whose destination
is clouded in mystery.
I feel if I have any
moral responsibility at all
it is to be happy,
provided I don't significantly harm someone.
And with this in mind
the choice becomes clear,
and I shall set out,
packing my best navigation gear,
into the great unknown.

Beacon

You're a distant memory
one I could easily forget.
But curiously enough
like a distant beacon
you still direct my life.
My feelings still locked
on the flickering flame
but I don't know
if I'll ever reach it.
I therefore hope
it either guide me home
or else extinguish itself;
leaving me to find
another beacon.

Hair

Her hair almost killed me.

Flowing like cascading rapids
over her shoulders.

I don't know why I fell
in love with her.
Was it her face,
her eyes,
her body,
her considerable intelligence,
or was it that mesmerizing hair?

It almost cost me
a year of medical school.

I was so love sick
after she dumped me
and had to sit in class
behind her
trying to listen
but all I could think about
was that Aphrodite's mane
could not be so magnificent.
So how could a mortal creature
be blessed with such beauty,
and sit there in front of me,
while I'm trying to concentrate,
killing me
with that goddamn
hair.

Deceased

It was not without warning-
with her advancing age,
frailty,
and ill health.
But when the end finally did come
it felt as abrupt as a car-wreck,
leaving me in shock
that a loved one could be permanently gone.
And as I sat that night
memories of her
kept invading my thoughts
even though she'd really left years ago
with her deteriorating mental state.
But her sweetness and good humor
lingered in my mind
and I said a prayer
that she be resting
in a warm and gentle place;
her health and youth restored
by divine benevolence.

Bitter

I read a poet the other day,
he sang not of affirmation
but rather condemnation.
Of alcohol,
of friendship,
of women,
of life.
The thoughts of a bitter old man.
And I was startled
and feared that once I get that old
I might be stricken with such venom also.
So I hope I might retain
enough love and achievement
to support my spirits
when my youth has long passed,
and let me mutter
with my last breath
an emphatic yes
to this earthly journey.

Poor Job

Like countless multitudes before him
he was given a test of faith.
Anchored to his belief
he was given one trial after another
until he cried out for death
and cursed his tortured state,
wondering what sins brought on such a fate.
Until one day the Lord did rescind
and bestowed great bounty upon him
for his loyalty and devotion.

Like him I have had a trial of faith,
it being bombarded like the winds shake the trees.
And I have tried to remain strong and true,
while my position and health were stripped away,
and though I wavered, once I committed
myself to believing in the higher good
the pounding stopped, revealing a path
that led me out of darkness, into a new beginning.

Racism

I don't know what makes
these people tick.
Spewing their venom
like a rabid snake.
Thinking that some people
should be killed
all because of the
color of their skin.

I know some would excuse
the harmless ones,
rationalizing it
as the product of
their upbringing in a small
prairie town.
But I find it inexcusable.
For these are precisely
the people that would have
owned slaves,
supported apartheid,
slaughtered the natives,
or condoned the holocaust.

And when I was
faced with this hatred
from a member of my family
I just remained silent.
Since I didn't see her often.
And I didn't want to be rude.

But later I wish I had
let her have it,
though I don't know
what difference it would make.
But someone has to stand up
in the name of decency
and common sense
before the atrocities start again.

I hope the next time
the person to stand up
will be me.

Unappreciated

I worked diligently for a year
crafting my verse,
studying the medium,
devoted to my muse,
which answered at regular intervals.
Until finally I felt ready
to toss my poems out to the world.
And later when I received
the eagerly anticipated reply
they just brushed me aside.
My most precious thoughts.
My deepest feelings.
And I mourned.
Deeply.
Shaken by this terrorist attack
on my dreams.
I didn't know
whether I should carry on.
I didn't want to continue
looking like the village idiot.
Then someone told me
most artists suffer rejection.
Some repeatedly.
Good ones.
So I decided
I was wedded
to this path
and forced myself
to write another poem

resigning to being
unappreciated
for a long
time.

Original

What's wrong with having
your own ideas?
They don't shoot you
for them here.
Although they sometimes
form a circle,
point their fingers
and laugh.
Particularly if you
were once one of them
and now would like to try
something new.
There is the danger of
being perceived as crazy.
So I try to reality test
my ideas on
a few people I can trust.
But as long as you're
not some nut
I don't see the why
you can't have your
own ideas
and vision.
Although this is probably
not uncommon.
The trick is to stick with it,
through the hard times.
Keep dialing the number
of your dreams,

even though its still busy.
Keep trying until you
get through or perish.
For this is what separates
the great from
the merely
mediocre.

Skyward

My poems all came back to me,
like light trying to escape a black hole,
so my star couldn't shine.
And I remain shrouded in darkness.
So I tinkered and repaired them
before I shot them skyward once more,
hoping they take their place in the heavens,
and send signals around the globe.

Whistle

Some get the call from outside.
The whine of the factory whistle
reminds them that its time
to put away their sandwiches and drinks,
butt out their cigarettes,
and make the long, deadening
march back to work.

I too have heard that whistle,
at fish camps where my hands froze,
and hospital wards where I cared for the sick.
But now the outer whistles have ceased
and my time is my own
due to the uncertain nature
of my mental health.

Happily, though, I also get
an inner call.
My internal whistle prompting me
to take up my writing.
Its a gentler call
allowing me flexibility of hours,
but its a call nonetheless
which must be answered
if my self esteem and happiness
are to remain intact.

Sensible

Its a typical retort
from her brand of bigot,
who thinks there can be
no other way
than the dogma of herself
and her friends.

Like a mule who has seen
it's first thoroughbred,
and demands he haul loads
like him, she demands
you conform to her
own narrow vision
of what work and the future
may hold; dismissing
your cherished dreams
as not being sensible,
while praising the same
characteristics in successful others.

I don't know how to
react to such attacks,
other than to go
about my work
with quiet determination;
and hope she not try
to sabotage things
if I eventually do
succeed.

Small Group

I was sick.
I couldn't concentrate.
Everywhere I looked
I saw her face.
All I could think about
was her infidelities.
The problem was
I was in a small group
in medical school
and was expected to be sharp
and attentive
and full of facts.

Well, I just couldn't do it.
As I became lightheaded
and started to sweat
I just bolted for the door,
leaving the scrutiny behind.

Later that night I reasoned
that my instructor was a doctor
so he would have empathy
for my lovesick condition.

How wrong I was.

Reminder

I was wandering the streets of Toronto-
visiting various stores, eating hot dogs,
sweating in the summer heat,
admiring the girls in jellied tank tops,
when I happened into a bookstore
and found myself in the poetry section.
As I flipped through the books,
and read the back covers,
I was told of the immense stature of the writers;
who were praised with uncompromising superlatives,
all intended to impress me-

and they did.

Until my own voice shriveled and cowered
and I wandered back into the bleak city streets,
surrounded by the business men in grey suits,
who seemed to laugh at my presumptuousness.
Thinking I could be a poet.
And I thought I should just get in line,
join the masses and don't stand out.

When I happened into another bookstore
and found Al Purdy stuffed in a bottom shelf.
As I read from the book I felt a booming voice shake me,
a belligerent roar shaking the porcelain pavement,
and he sang out to me,
"There can be no better life than to write poems.

Don't you believe this to be so?"
And I nodded my head silently,
knowing I could not conceive it to be otherwise.

Normal

Its a funny little word,
one that most take for granted.
Meaning of sound mind and body.
Which includes a wide range
of human behaviors;
but doesn't include my experience.

I was of the most unsound mind,
certifiably crazy,
and was rightfully carted away
and treated with medicine.

Happily, now I can say
I am normal,
with the dragons, demons, and witches
defeated by my pills,
and my mood given
a much needed boost.
So I can say I feel normal,
and happy,
confident that life's little joys
will not be denied me any longer.

Insoluble

Its an insoluble problem
as far as I can see:
How do I get a girlfriend?
Oh, I know, some might say the bars,
but they have never been my thing,
or the personals,
but they are too risky, like a blind date,
or friends,
but I don't have many left.
And all these things are ill suited
to one who is introspective
and quiet, and prefers his
own company a lot of the time.
Like a fly caught in a house
I probably don't know
how far I am from where I should be
and if I'll ever get there again.
So all I can do is pray
to God,
to Aphrodite,
to Marilyn Monroe
to find me someone soon;
before age sets in
wasting my sexual prime.

Realistic

I hate dreaming.
It gives me heartburn
and fills my head
with crazy ideas
of fame and it's
embellishments
when I know full well
that only a small percentage
of people reach that
pinnacle, leaving the
rest to scramble to
build mundane lives,
like shoppers raiding
a bargain bin.
So I'll try to be realistic,
hedge my bets,
and tell myself
"it can always be
  your hobby"
while doing the
best I can to scale
that peak.

In a Silent Way

I don't know when it was
I realized I didn't fit in.
It surely was at a young age, though.
As the kids laughed and played
I felt strangely different
and was frequently left out.
As I got older it just got worse.
I thought I had a social lesion
that kept me from fitting in
and painfully sought my own company.
As an adult now, I still find
socialization difficult. I prefer
my own company, but unlike a
hermit or a recluse, I treasure
the few key people I choose
to have in my life.
And I'm finally coming to see
my silent, soft-spoken disposition
as healthy, rather than a defect.

Hidden

Why must I hide it?
Stuff my papers between my mattress,
close the curtains tight when I work,
afraid someone will discover who I am.
Cling to a regular job
just to prove something to my parents.
That is I can work and function
like a regular human being,
when I'm not regular.
I'm a writer, an artist
and have the means to support myself,
but until I get published
I have to feign this normality;
hiding my true identity
like the sun hides the stars.

Mistress

I did what I had to do.
Got up, shaved,
put on my tie and coat,
and drove through traffic
to the inner city hospital
where I was to start my job,
my medical job,
with the eminent psychiatrist.
And I sat while he interviewed a patient
and tried to do my ratings.
But my thoughts kept drifting
to poetry, music,
and you.
The things I care about.
The things I have passion for.
And I wondered what I was doing there
and why I still try to think
of myself as a doctor at all
when my heart is firmly somewhere else.
I think its not fair
to both myself and the patients
since I have a different mistress,
one I'm mad about,
so I should probably end it,
if I could just bow out gracefully.

Focus

It was only after I'd
thrown out what I didn't need,
avoided what I didn't want,
pieced together what I truly desired,
let my passion rule the day,
and tore up the rules as they'd been played
that I was able to truly focus,
like an eagle in pursuit,
on the task at hand.
Channeling my energy
to serve my goals
I felt a grace came over me
as the words did flow
and I knew that someday
I would succeed.
Through persistence
like the grass that continues to grow,
even though its continually cut,
or the sun that defeats the darkness
every morning.

Denial

I don't want to think about it,
not the depth of your love,
nor the affection in your touch,
not the sweetness of your smile,
nor the aroma of your hair.
For you see I've had enough
of these daydreams and midnight longings.
So I must deny
what I feel for you,
how you moved me
with such precious little time.
Yes, I must deny
what you mean to me
until your memory fades
or by some chance
our lives do meet again.

War

It seems so senseless.
Or so it seems to me,
my having no direct
experience with it,
having lived in a stable
peaceful country all my life.
But the images of war
That I am all to familiar with
make me wonder what it is
that possesses a group of men
to devise new ways to kill humans.
Like the gas chamber,
or the crucifix.
Perhaps it is in the war against evil,
like the makers of the first atomic bomb,
but mostly it is just petty trash
that drives the arms makers and merchants
who supply the young men,
who sacrifice it all,
for some trivial issue.
And leave women widowed
and children orphaned.
A pain I cannot conceive of to bear.
No, in our part of the world
crime is the only problem,
but that has never really touched me;
even though the tools of war
are in their hands too.

Smarts

I am one of the smartest
people I know.
The problem is
there are some
who disagree.
This would be alright
except that they mock me,
belittling my dreams and vision,
saying I don't have
what it takes,
that I lack the required
intelligence and talent.

Could I be so wrong?

Only time will tell
whether like an oasis
in the desert,
my vision turns out
to be all too false;
or like the sighting
of land to Columbus
my vision steers me true,
revealing rich new lands.

Chaotic

They say its chaotic-
the id or unconscious.
A seething cauldron of images
bubbling to the surface
and disturbing periodically
what we like to perceive as our
rational, orderly minds.

Well, I say its orderly also.
In fact, more orderly
than our conscious minds.
For is not nature orderly?
Are dreams chaotic?
Undecipherable sometimes yes,
but not chaotic.

This source of poetry,
of insights ahead of
the conscious mind,
must possess a clarity
and utility beyond
mere chaos.

Or life would be one
chaotic mess.
And from where I sit
it clearly is not.

Desperation

I've been locked out for years,
watching them dance under the moonlight,
seeing them retire to love-struck rooms,
my illness shackling me from breaking through.
And as I sit watching them sweep up afterwards
I'm lonely and wanting one more time,
and I wonder about the few left with me-
surely not the object of my ardent desire,
but could they make me soar again?
Or are just decoys to my true bliss?
I doubt they could truly heal me,
for out of desperation is born the seeds of sadness
and such affairs just confuse the lives of men.

Preference

She's so damn intransigent,
I've told her my feelings,
outlined my likes and dislikes,
said what I'd prefer to avoid
but still she makes me face head on
that which I've done before
and don't particularly enjoy
and like a soldier who's forced to march
when he'd rather be with his sweetheart.
I'm bitter,
and confused
and feel I'm a better judge
of my time and activities
then her, however well intentioned
she may be.

Sensitivity

She takes the knife
out of it's sheath
and with a few offhand
remarks about my inactivity
and errant ways
it feels as if the knife
is thrust upwards into my stomach.
It seizing like a knot.
After she's gone
the knot remains,
and I go over her words,
again and again in my head,
crafting replies in vain.
My sensitivity exposed
like a quivering, raw nerve.
And I don't know how
to shake it off,
only after do I realize,
and hour or so later,
that it was not meant
with malice; and I
overreacted like a mother
to the sight of blood,
then the knot disappears;
so I can clear my mind,
and mount a rational defense.

Tolerance

She can't stand the way I do things
and its the little things the most
that upset her in their deviance
from her cherished standards and norms.
So I tell her its not a problem.
I'm just different than she is,
not abnormal, just dissimilar.
But she shakes her head,
and wags her finger
at my subversive behavior
and I pray she learn some tolerance
and the wisdom of accepting that
which is not like yourself.

Diagnosis

They said I have an illness,
with mood swings and psychosis,
but I know things are different-
for although I get sick,
my sickness is a battle
with dragons, ogres and demons
and the only way to respond
is to be heroic.
I know this is no typical illness.
But notwithstanding I take my pills,
and endure the diagnostic label,
knowing full well I will be branded
this way for life;
and must carry my true identity
close to my heart.

Balance

She gives me balance
like snow to a forest.
Gone are the days
of purely masculine pursuits.
Instead a softer, gentler touch
accompanies my harder ways
and I can enjoy greater harmony
and a more robust nature.

Like the Moon

While the womanly god demands our veneration, the godlike woman kindles our love; but while we allow ourselves to melt in the celestial loveliness, the celestial self-sufficiency holds us back in awe.

Friedrich Von Schiller

So far and yet so close
She takes my breath away.
Her eyes sparkle like diamonds,
and Her hair hangs in ringlets
which caress Her bosom.
The sea, the moon, the stars
express Her great beauty.
Leaving me to see for the first time
the bounty of Nature
and adore Her loving hand
as it caresses my weary heart.
Listening as She whispers-
the verse from Her my Muse.
Once Her's, I'm lost forever,
though soon She's near me
and I'm fine.

Magic

She makes me smile
with her magical ways.
My heart beats faster
as she unfolds her erotic delights.
No one knows she loves me
but we know it all too well
and steal away to share our love
under charmed skies.
Soon she will be with me
and forever by my side,
my heart laughing joyfully
with my only bride.

Cross

Its a sick symbol
depicting a crucified God,
self sacrifice,
and suffering.
I don't know how they
came up with such a thing,
and what it says about
God, man and life.
But I do know it
corrupts minds
and souls
into believing God's bounty
is not to be enjoyed.
So I pray for those under it's spell;
that they may some day wake up,
get down off the cross,
and start enjoying things.
Like we were meant to do.

To the Heavens

Oh, brilliant nighttime sky,
with your endless emeralds and beauty,
you're like a timeless woman
whose charm never ceases to amaze.
Unfold your mysteries for me
and let me see them for the first time
amazed, yet reverent
at the distances between us.
I look to see your secrets
and see revealed the face of eternity.
A timeless vision that endures
with nothing out of place.
Save for me a place in heaven,
and I'll gaze at you lovingly,
while I'm here on earth.

Identity

We didn't share much together,
just a few words and a dance,
but it left me mesmerized
with who you are
leaving me to wonder if you
really possessed the attributes
I thought you did.
Now that its apparent
I will never see you again
I'm curious about the real you.
Are you an exceptional woman?
Or was that just my mind's
interpretation of our brief encounter.
I guess I'll never know
and must carry this ghost
of a woman with me
until someone takes her place;
and the knowledge of your mediocrity
extinguishes the flame that now burns for you.

Bad

Let's talk about devils.
First there's the Luciferian kind.
These cringing, petty tyrants
who ironically use the cross as their symbol
and have terrorized mankind for two millenniums.
They turn fun into sin,
are filled with hate,
and are just plain evil.

Then there's the Mephistophelean kind,
the spirit of sexual energy and adventure.
And they're bad,
very bad.
The things they would like to do
to women would make an
Evangelist see red,
but they bring delight
to their female partners.
They live in the heart of
every man, and have been
abused for too long.

Which one would you choose?
Which one would you persecute?

Lazy

I strung up a hammock today
as the days got endlessly long
and hot, like a desert sagebrush
and I climbed in to do sweet nothing
but just gaze up at the sky,
watching the treetops sway,
and the leaves glisten,
as serene as a calm lake,
and hoped no one
would come for me until
I welcomed the dense, starry night.
Just me me and my thoughts
meandering slowly,
and lazily,
under the sun.

Stethoscope

She was just a young girl,
a toddler really,
yet there she was
coughing up green phlegm,
with a fever.
So I took out my stethoscope
with it's toy bunny
wrapped around it's neck,
gently pressing it against her chest.
As I squeezed her hand
and asked her to breath
in and out
as I listened.
I heard no pneumonia
so I placed her on antibiotics
for her bronchitis.
I didn't know if it
would stop her getting sicker,
but I hoped my stethoscope
might lift her spirits,
and help her heal.

Vampire

She'll suck you bone dry
of you let her.
Half dead she wanders this earth,
depending on the comfort of others,
dumping her problems,
clinging to their empathy,
lacking the courage to stand alone
or face the daylight head on.
So she slinks in the darkness
desperate,
and needy.

Evolution

I've heard the creation myths
sing of a divine spark.
I've heard the evolutionary theories
speak of random mutations.
But if not only form but beauty
reigns supreme in the natural world,
and this planet is exquisitely
balanced and fine tuned,
it must be we were designed
out of more than sheer necessity
but also with an artist's touch
which could not create something
out of nothing.
But had to do it gradually-
mixing the genetic makeups,
like an artist mixes paints;
for it seems to me
evolution is how God creates.

Lassitude

The right sort of woman can distinguish between Creative Lassitude and plain shiftlessness.

Robertson Davies

She says I'm inactive
and should do more.
Why can't she see
I'm active in my head?
For while sitting in a chair,
or lying on my bed,
I'm constantly turning over
a wide variety of subjects
like a craftsman his materials,
until I get an idea
or insight
that becomes a poem;
or perhaps something paltry.
And though I don't
have calluses on my hands
I have plenty between the ears
and work very hard
in the guise of a loaf.

Sculptor

Your words live on
inside my head,
mostly the criticism
although sometimes
in the right mood
some praise comes through.

You try to mold me
like a sculptor his clay
but this clay has different ideas
and resists your chiseling
returning to an unformed mass
before it tries to resurrect itself
by its own hand.

Some day I hope to silence
your voice in my head,
primarily to stop the criticism,
but also so I can hear you
clearly, unfiltered, without the
amplification of a child's fear;
and accept you as the priceless ally
you now are.

Mother

She's bound to me,
like the hummingbird to the rose,
or the straightjacket to the lunatic;
and is at times nurturing
or just plain restrictive.
So I have sometimes tried to break free
and sang my independence
under the midnight moon
like a junk yard dog.
Only to return again
to the familiar porch light
with it's well known kitchen,
home cooked meals,
and inquisitive probings
of all the intricate
details of my life.
But I'll never give up
my struggle
to implement my vision
of who I want to be;
while accepting this bond,
the strength of which
could weather any storm,
or endure any hardship.

Alchemy

I wore blue,
the color of dignity.

She wore red,
for her passionate nature.

We shared a drink
under the springtime stars.

Later our bodies transformed
desire into motion

and she let me touch heaven
until we split apart again.

Climbing Mount Hippocrates

Its a steep climb
with missteps,
ups and downs,
and obstacles.
The weather is sometimes foul
and some never make it.
Hard work
pays off in the end though
and for those who
persist in climbing
her cliffs
the cherished degree
is rewarded at the end.
The sense of accomplishment
at planting your flag
at the summit
with it's feelings of
mastery and endurance
is something you can
carry with you the rest
of your life.
Like the title,
the diploma
on your wall,
and the good habits,
of real world problem solving,
you developed.

Transition

I was happily on my way,
surrounded by my friends,
when suddenly I was attacked
by a wild boar-
who chased me into the bush,
and after much difficulty,
I managed to slay the beast.
Finding no tracks
or path
to guide me back
I cried for help
only to find my companions
had deserted me.
I was then left with the decision
whether to go back
to the known and familiar,
or to forge ahead
to new and unexpected.
I decided on the riskier path,
took out my compass,
and set out in the bush.
I found it not easy going,
and like an adolescent
stuck between childhood
and maturity,
I didn't quite know exactly
what the end product would be.
But I vowed to endure

the difficulties
and uncertainties
of a life in
transition.

Nerves

It gets you in your gut.
Feeling as though you swallowed
a mouthful of pins and needles
that churn in your stomach
or if it gets worse
as if you swallowed a jagged edge.
And then your mind locks onto
that which you'd prefer to avoid-
a commitment that causes you distress.
And you turn it over in your head
wringing your hands and asking
"Do I really have to do it?
 Will I slip on a banana peel
   as I enter the meeting?"
More likely than not you
do have to do it
and try to see the benefits
of completing the task,
aiming for your average performance,
hitting the mark,
and engaging before
your stomach hemorrhages
to death.

Slaughter

The beast was inside of me,
overpowering my defenses.
Taking over my will
until I foamed like a rabid dog
and lashed out at my loved ones,
almost striking them physically.

There was only one alternative -
it must be slaughtered,
the beast dismembered.
And they did,
tying me down,
injecting me with medicine
until he finally died.
And I could reconstitute myself,
like a dried up lake,
in the runoff after a drought.

Sparkle

It never leaves me alone.
Not when I think,
not when I eat,
not when I write,
not when I retire at night.
And I don't want to think
about it too much
because it invariably
turns to time spans
and opportunities long lost
and the great chasm
of a distance between me
and success with
the opposite sex.

So I obsess about my appearance
and buy new clothes
and try to think where to go
where a lonely introvert
might get a break.
And pray that when it does come
the words come out right,
and my soul still possesses
the sparkle of worth
it once possessed
so many years
ago.

Hat

It sits perched upon my dresser,
with it's stiff rim
and indented felt crown.
Reminding me
that I must
above all think,
be analytical,
like a newspaper reporter.
Yielding to no theory
unless it possesses truth,
seeing things through
the glasses of a realist;
which in no was supersedes
the life of my imagination.
Keeping me anchored,
both feet on the ground,
hat on my head,
able to soar to new heights
and come home to a smooth landing.

Starting Anew

It was a most modest start,
just a passing interest really.
But when I committed
the desire rose
with each completed task
until it consumed me
like the rush of sexual satisfaction.
And I vowed to become competent
by practice and study,
my life being rejuvenated
by my newfound goal;
like a first grader
after he's settled in.

The Eternal All-Inclusive

Its identity is kept quite secret
although for most of humanity
it was believed in by most.

Nowadays it is scarcely considered,
with the atheism of modern times,
where people only expect earthly rewards.
And assault life like a raging bull,
trying to force their will on others,
thinking all there is to be is here.

Well, why not consider happiness?
This earthly journey being far too short,
with most people getting things together
only to find themselves old.

Consider a place beyond here
where youth and health is restored
to the good hearted and just,
where happiness on all levels,
including that of the mind,
is bestowed by the Lord
in a place of intense beauty.
Where all the assholes are gone,
and you spend your days
in eternal bliss
with the best people
mankind has ever produced.

The Fall of Prometheus

So much has happened
on this planet.
The slow march of history
betraying many lessons,
and mistakes made
over and over again.

Yet people today
think history began
with the birth
of the television
and the major events
of the 20th century.

The supremacy of science
as the source of answers
to most people
I foresee melting away,
as all the attainable answers
are figured out one day
in the future.
And like a detective
who has collected
all the possible facts
pure science will
fizzle out and die
as an investigative endeavor.
Leaving us with its greatest gift
the marvels of technology.

It is then that the words
of the old poets and philosophers
will sing again for people,
with the celebration
of nature, art and spirituality
coming back like the tides,
restoring meaning to this world,
balancing the accomplishments
of science with the
lessons of history.
Making enriching life on this earth
the goal of humanity
rather than reaching
for the stars.

Silence

Like a meadow under starlit skies
She lies as tranquil as a a lake.
The strip-malls and industry
drive Her deep beneath the sea,
while a chain of power-lines over forests
are a crown of thorns upon Her hair.
Subjecting things to inspection
while teasing them apart with dissection,
the soul of the earth recedes
until it is found as faint as a whisper.
But like the crisp streams
of a spring runoff
She shall one day return;
while beyond the coarse hands
of stumbling Science
She sits in silence.

About the Author

Paul Kloschinsky was born in Saskatchewan in 1963. He received a B.Sc. in Computer Science as well as an MD from the University of British Columbia in the 1980's. He has worked as a General Practitioner for a time. For a period in the past he suffered mental health problems as outlined in his first book of poems A Time To Cry. In addition to being a writer, he is also an avid songwriter and photographer. He now lives in Delta, BC. This is his second book.

He has a website at www.kloschinsky.com.

ISBN 142511731-7